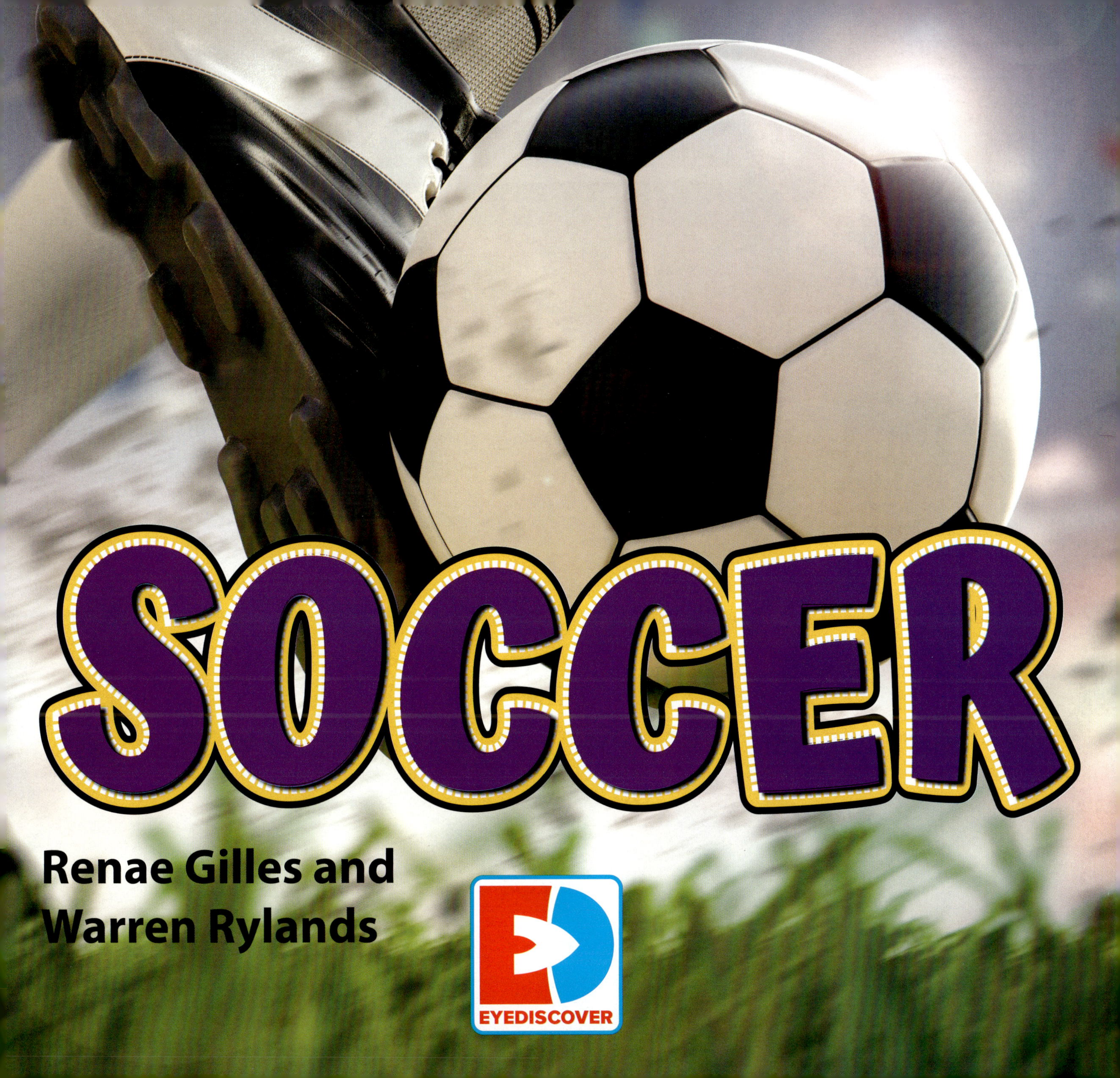

SOCCER

Renae Gilles and
Warren Rylands

Go to **www.eyediscover.com** and enter this book's unique code.

BOOK CODE

AVA78647

EYEDISCOVER brings you optic readalongs that support active learning.

Published by AV² by Weigl
350 5th Avenue, 59th Floor New York, NY 10118
Website: www.eyediscover.com

Library of Congress Control Number: 2018951113

ISBN 978-1-4896-8034-1 (hardcover)

Printed in the United States of America
in Brainerd, Minnesota
1 2 3 4 5 6 7 8 9 0 22 21 20 19 18

082018
120917

Project Coordinator: John Willis
Designer: Mandy Christiansen

Weigl acknowledges Alamy, Getty Images, and iStock as the primary image suppliers for this title.

EYEDISCOVER provides enriched content, optimized for tablet use, that supplements and complements this book. EYEDISCOVER books strive to create inspired learning and engage young minds in a total learning experience.

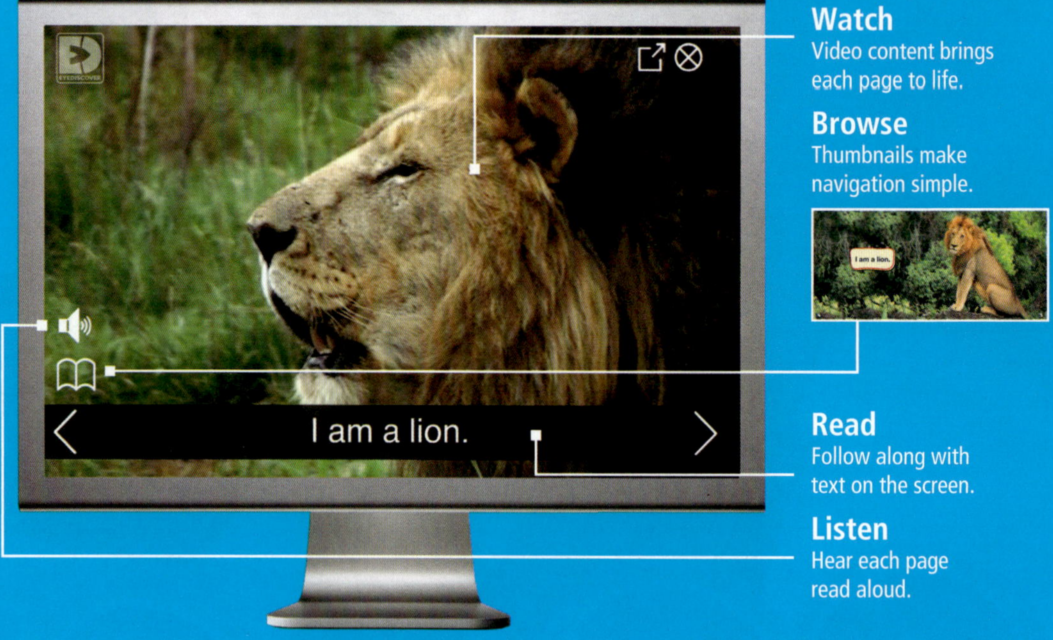

Watch
Video content brings each page to life.

Browse
Thumbnails make navigation simple.

Read
Follow along with text on the screen.

Listen
Hear each page read aloud.

Your EYEDISCOVER Optic Readalongs come alive with...

Audio
Listen to the entire book read aloud.

Video
High resolution videos turn each spread into an optic readalong.

OPTIMIZED FOR
- TABLETS
- WHITEBOARDS
- COMPUTERS
- AND MUCH MORE!

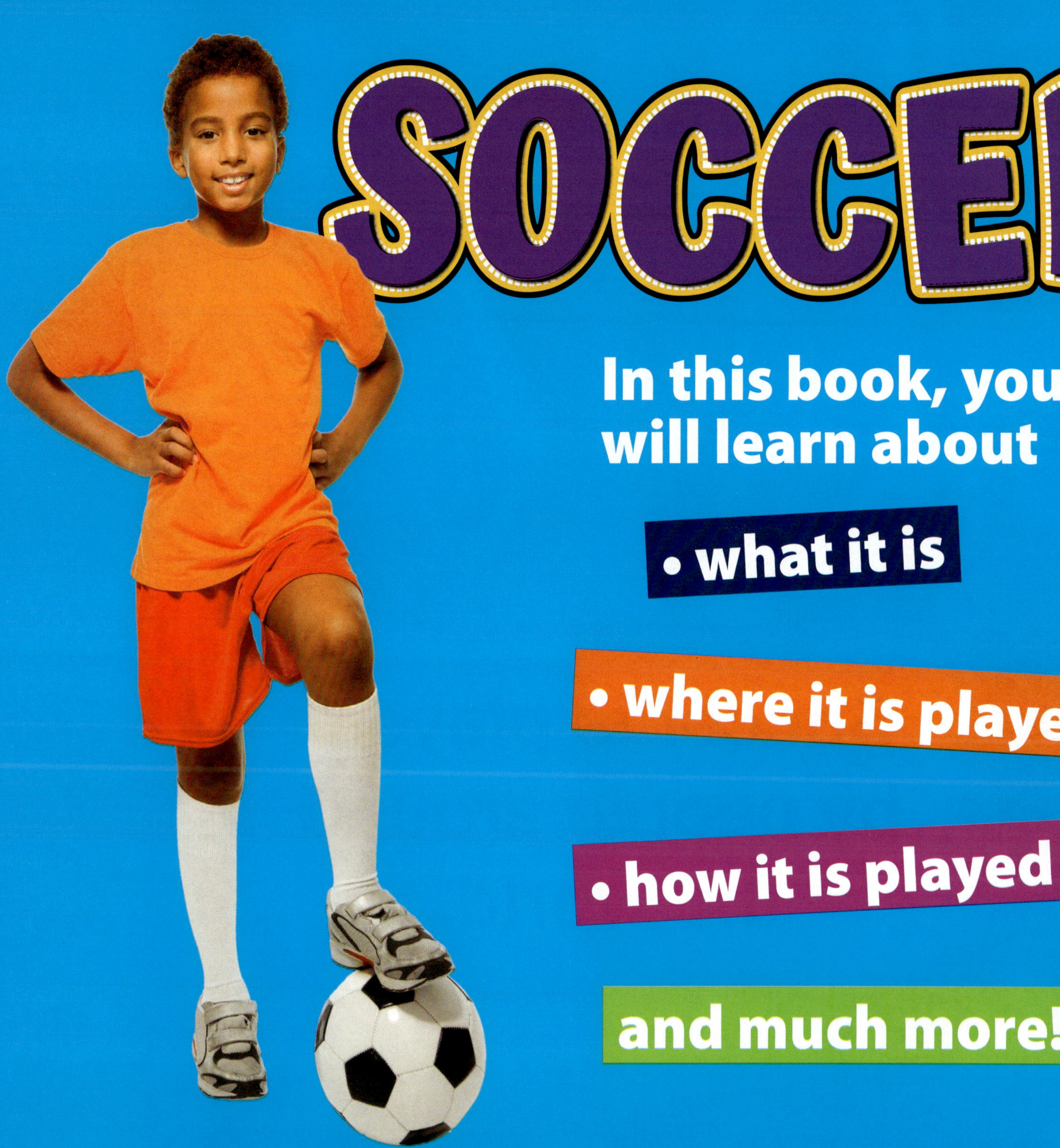

SOCCER

In this book, you will learn about

- what it is
- where it is played
- how it is played

and much more!

Soccer is played by people around the world.

2018 FIFA WORLD CUP RUSSIA
#worldcup
2018 FIFA WORLD CUP RUSSIA
МОСКВА
FIFA

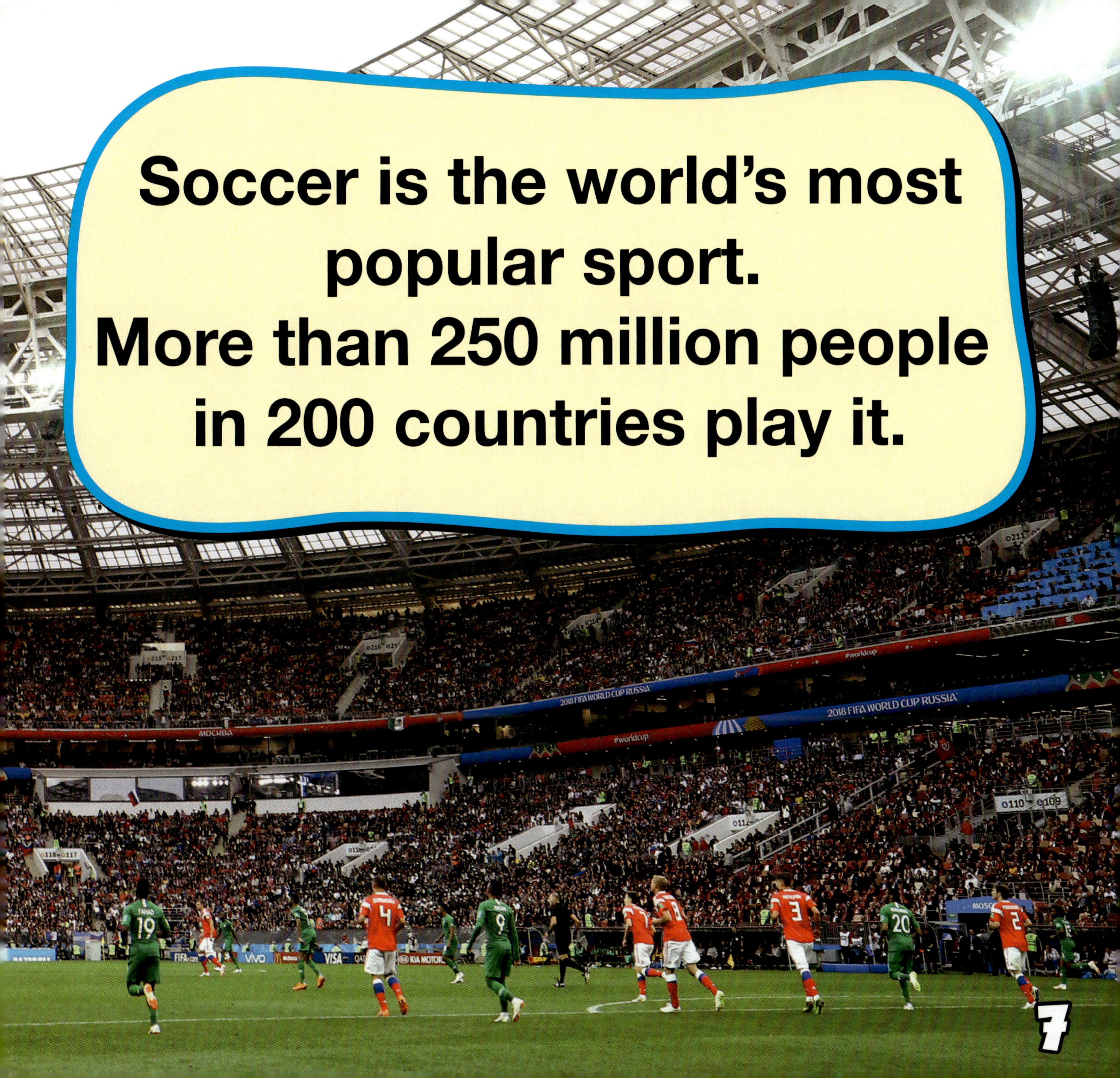

Soccer is the world's most popular sport. More than 250 million people in 200 countries play it.

Soccer is played while running on foot. People in many countries call it “football.”

Players score by kicking the ball into the other team's goal.

Only goalkeepers can use their hands. They can catch and throw the ball.

There are 23 Major League Soccer teams in the United States.

NEW YORK

A group called FIFA holds a World Cup tournament every four years. The World Cup trophy is made of solid gold.

The FIFA World Cup is the most watched sports event in the world.

AUF ZUR TITELVERTEIDIGUNG
Mind your manners.
Mind your manners.
Mind your manners.
Mercedes-Benz
EPPINGEN
COMMERZBANK
Die Bank an Ihrer Seite

People make many good friends when they play soccer together.

SOCCER BY THE NUMBERS

More than **3 billion** people watch the **World Cup** each year.

The **MLS** started in **1996.**

Brazil has won the **FIFA World Cup five** times.

Most soccer games are **90 minutes** long.

The **fastest** soccer kick was **80.1 miles** per hour.

(128.9 kilometers per hour)

Usually only **two** or three **goals** are scored in a soccer game.

KEY WORDS

Research has shown that as much as 65 percent of all written material published in English is made up of 300 words. These 300 words cannot be taught using pictures or learned by sounding them out. They must be recognized by sight. This book contains 37 common sight words to help young readers improve their reading fluency and comprehension. This book also teaches young readers several important content words, such as proper nouns. These words are paired with pictures to aid in learning and improve understanding.

Page	Sight Words First Appearance
4	around, by, is, people, the, world
7	in, it, more, most, play, than
8	call, many, on, while
10	into, other
13	and, can, only, their, they, use
14	are, there
16	a, every, four, group, made, of, years
21	good, make, together, when

Page	Content Words First Appearance
4	soccer
7	countries, million, people, sport
8	foot, football
10	ball, goal, kicking, score, team
13	goalkeepers, hands
14	league, United States
16	FIFA, gold, tournament, trophy, World Cup
21	friends

Watch
Video content brings each page to life.

Browse
Thumbnails make navigation simple.

Read
Follow along with text on the screen.

Listen
Hear each page read aloud.

Go to www.eyediscover.com and enter this book's unique code.

BOOK CODE

AVA78647